Plain Sailing

By
Deirdre Dermody

Illustrated by
Salvacion Delos Reyes

Information for instructors

This series of books is designed for children who have learned the **vowel digraphs** or **vowel teams** (e.g. ai, oa, ie) and would benefit from practising or revising them. These books also incorporate many **High Frequency Words** (HFWs) and sight words. HFWs account for more than half of the words in children's books. The ability to instantly recognise these words will enable children to read with **greater fluency and confidence.**

A useful phrase in regard to vowel digraphs is the following: *when two vowels go walking the first one sometimes does the talking and it usually says its name*. This book focuses on the 'ai' digraph, 'ai' says the letter name or long /a/ as in sail. These digraphs have been highlighted in blue to make them instantly recognisable. The vowels are a, e, i, o & u but please note the letter y sometimes behaves as a vowel (e.g. ay as in play).The magic e also features in this series. A rhyme for this is: *magic e plays a game it makes the vowel say its name* e.g. the long /a/ sound in lake. The vowel and magic e are highlighted in red in the book.

Splitting up longer words can help children to decode them e.g. fish-ing or tool-box. Words which have been split or contain magic e can be found at the top of some pages to allow readers to decode them prior to reading the text. This encourages more fluent reading of the page.

Farm Phonics also utilises thinking strategies such as Making Predictions, Visualisation, Making Connections and Questioning to **improve comprehension.** The instructor and child may engage in conversations about the books using these questions as prompts.

The learning can also be extended to include **oral language and writing** by having the child discuss possible endings for the story and create their own endings either orally, pictorially or in writing.

For more information and resources please go to
www.vibrantyoungminds.ie

FAMILY TREE

Pat

Mim

Gail

Jack

Liam

Max

Ella

Tess

Sam

What do you think the story will be about?

Visualisations

Pretend you are on a lake. What can you see, hear and smell?

Sound Words - ai

plain

sail

sailing

hail

pail

bail

bailing

aid

drain

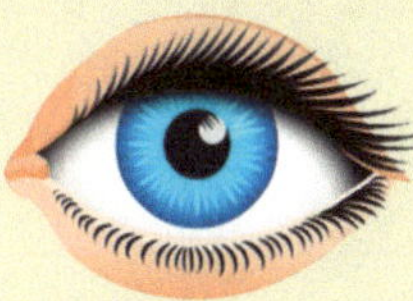

there	get
from	go
what	look
was	no
on	up
did	you
of	him
will	see

It was a good day on the farm. Pat did lots of farming.

Tess is with Pat. They are at the lake.

They will get in the boat
and go fishing.

They pull off from the
dock.

Making Connections

What things do you like to do to relax?
Tell me about a book that was about the outdoors?
What do you know about fishing?

Pat is fishing. It is fun.
He is looking at the big
birds.

What is Tess looking at?

She spots a problem and
starts to bark!

There is a hole in the boat!

There is no plug!

Pat jumps up. He gets his pail.

Pat starts bailing water out of the boat.

How did the hole get into boat?

How does Pat feel?

What happens next?

Jack and Liam are on
the lake.

They can see Pat and
Tess. Pat waves his arms
to hail them.

Can they aid him?

The men are twins.
Liam fixes cars and vans.
He has his toolbox
with him.

"What is the problem?"
he asks.

Liam has a spare drain plug. "Take this", says Liam.

Pat puts it in the hole.

Jack ties a rope on to
Pat's boat.

Pat and Tess get on to
the boat with the twins.

"Thank you for helping
us" says Pat. Tess wags
her tail.

Possible Endings
Pat fixes
the boat.
They go
for a spin.
Pat calls
Mim.

Create your own ending to the story
Who is in the ending?
Where are they?
What do they do?

29

Published in 2021
by Vibrant Young Minds Publishing

By
Deirdre Dermody

Illustrated by
Salvacion Delos Reyes

ISBN 978-1-9168801-1-5